100

things you should know about

MAMMALS

100

things you should know about

MAMMALS

Jinny Johnson
Consultant: Steve Parker

Miles Kelly
PUBLISHING

First published in 2004 by
Miles Kelly Publishing Ltd
Bardfield Centre, Great Bardfield, Essex, CM7 4SL

Copyright © Miles Kelly Publishing 2004

2 4 6 8 10 9 7 5 3

Editorial Director: Belinda Gallagher
Art Director: Jo Brewer
Project Editor: Neil de Cort
Volume Designer: Sally Lace
Picture Researcher: Liberty Newton
Indexer, Proof Reader: Janet De Saulles
Production Manager: Elizabeth Brunwin

ISBN 1-84236-351-4

Printed in China

ACKNOWLEDGEMENTS

The Publishers would like to thank the following artists who have
contributed to this book:

Chris Buzer/ Studio Galante
Luca Di Castri/ Studio Galante
Jim Channell/ Bernard Thornton
Illustration
Mike Foster/ Maltings Partnership
Wayne Ford
Chris Forsey
L.R. Galante/ Studio Galante
Brooks Hagan/ Studio Galante
Emma Louise Jones
Roger Kent

Stuart Lafford/ Linden Artists
Kevin Maddison
Alan Male/ Linden Artists
Janos Marffy
Massimiliano Maugeri/ Studio Galante
Colin Newman/ Bernard Thornton
Illustration
Eric Robson/ Illustration Limited
Mike Saunders
Francesco Spadoni/ Studio Galante
Christian Webb/ Temple Rogers

Cartoons by Mark Davis at Mackerel

www.mileskelly.net
info@mileskelly.net

Contents

What are mammals?

1 **Mammals are warm-blooded animals with a bony skeleton and fur or hair.** Being warm-blooded means that a mammal can keep its body at a constant temperature, even if the weather is very cold. The skeleton supports the body and protects the delicate parts inside, such as the heart, lungs and brain. There is one sort of mammal you know very well, it's you!

African savanna elephant

Eurasian beaver

Meerkat

European water vole

Eurasian otter

Cheetah

Red panda

Greater
fruit bat

Lion

Greater
horseshoe
bat

Western tarsier

Racoon-dog

The mammal world

2 There are nearly 4500 different types of mammal. Most have babies which grow inside the mother's body. While a baby mammal grows, a special organ called a placenta supplies it with food and oxygen from the mother's body. These mammals are called placental mammals.

▼ This echidna is part of a group of mammals called monotremes. They do not give birth to live young – they lay eggs instead.

4 Not all mammals' young develop inside the mother's body. Two smaller groups of mammals do things differently. Monotremes, like platypuses and echidnas or spiny anteaters, lay eggs. The platypus lays her eggs in a burrow, but the echidna keeps her single egg in a special dip in her belly until it is ready to hatch

▼ Duck-billed platypus

3 Mammal mothers feed their babies on milk from their own bodies. The baby sucks this milk from teats on special mammary glands, also called udders or breasts, on the mother's body. The milk contains all the food the young animal needs to help it grow.

▲ Olive baboons live in Africa in groups called troops of between 20 and 150 animals.

5 **Marsupials give birth to tiny young that finish developing in a pouch.** A baby kangaroo is only 2 centimetres long when it is born. Tiny, blind and hairless, it makes its own way to the safety of its mother's pouch. Once there, it latches onto a teat in the pouch and begins to feed.

▲ The baby kangaroo stays in the pouch for about six months while it grows.

▲ Fallow deer have a good sense of smell, and excellent sight.

6 **Most mammals have good senses of sight, smell and hearing.** Their senses help them watch out for enemies, find food and keep in touch with each other. For many mammals, smell is their most important sense. Plant-eaters such as rabbits and deer sniff the air for signs of danger such as the scent of a predator.

Big and small

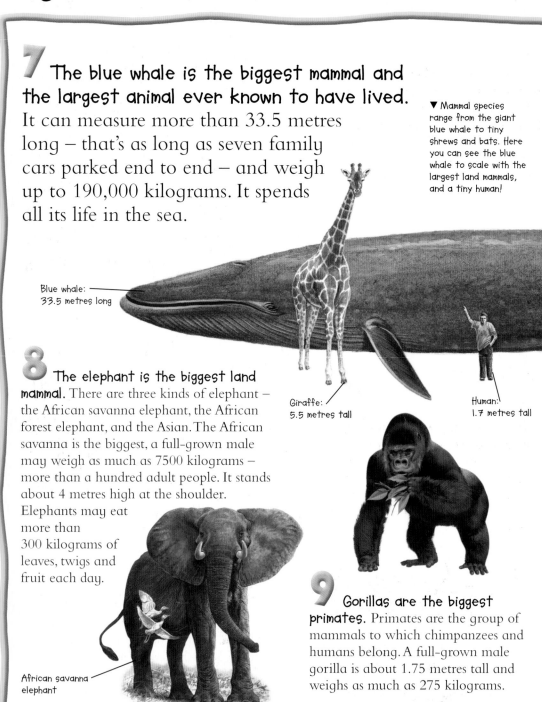

7 **The blue whale is the biggest mammal and the largest animal ever known to have lived.** It can measure more than 33.5 metres long – that's as long as seven family cars parked end to end – and weigh up to 190,000 kilograms. It spends all its life in the sea.

▼ Mammal species range from the giant blue whale to tiny shrews and bats. Here you can see the blue whale to scale with the largest land mammals, and a tiny human!

Blue whale:
33.5 metres long

8 **The elephant is the biggest land mammal.** There are three kinds of elephant – the African savanna elephant, the African forest elephant, and the Asian. The African savanna is the biggest, a full-grown male may weigh as much as 7500 kilograms – more than a hundred adult people. It stands about 4 metres high at the shoulder. Elephants may eat more than 300 kilograms of leaves, twigs and fruit each day.

Giraffe:
5.5 metres tall

Human:
1.7 metres tall

African savanna elephant

9 **Gorillas are the biggest primates.** Primates are the group of mammals to which chimpanzees and humans belong. A full-grown male gorilla is about 1.75 metres tall and weighs as much as 275 kilograms.

10 The giraffe is the tallest of all the mammals. A male giraffe is about 5.5 metres tall – that's more than three or four people standing on each other's shoulders. The giraffe lives in Africa, south of the Sahara desert. Its height helps it reach fresh juicy leaves at the tops of trees.

Brown bear:
2.4 metres tall

African elephant:
4 metres tall

11 The capybara is the largest living rodent. Rodents are the group of mammals that include rats and mice. At about 1.3 metres long the capybara is a giant compared to most rodents. It lives around ponds, lakes and rivers in South America.

12 The smallest mammal in the world is the tiny hog–nosed bat. A full-grown adult's body is only 3 centimetres long. It weighs about 2 grams – less than a teaspoon of rice!

13 The tiny mouse deer is only the size of a hare. Also known as the chevrotain, this little creature is only about 85 centimetres long and stands about 30 centimetres high at the shoulder. It lives in African forests.

Fast movers

14 **The cheetah can run faster than any other animal.** It can move at about 100 kilometres an hour, but it cannot run this fast for long. The cheetah uses its speed to catch other animals to eat. It creeps towards its prey until it is only about 100 metres away. Then it races towards it at top speed, ready for the final attack.

▲ The cheetah's long slender legs and muscular body help it to run fast. The long tail balances the body while it is running.

15 The red kangaroo is a champion jumper. It can leap along at 40 kilometres an hour or more. The kangaroo needs to be able to travel fast. It lives in the dry desert lands of Australia and often has to journey long distances to find grass to eat and water to drink.

▼ The pronghorn is one of the fastest mammals in North America. It has to run to escape its enemies, such as wolves.

▲ The red kangaroo can leap 9 or 10 metres in a single bound.

17 The pronghorn is slower than the cheetah, but it can run for longer. It can keep up a speed of 70 kilometres an hour for about ten minutes.

16 Even the little brown hare can run at more than 70 kilometres an hour. Its powerful back legs help it move fast enough to escape enemies such as foxes.

SPEED DEMONS!
How do you compare to the fastest mammal on earth? Ask an adult to measure how far you can run in 10 seconds. Times this by 6, and then times the answer by 60 to find out how many metres you can run in an hour. If you divide this by 1000 you will get your speed in kilometres per hour. You will find it will be far less than the cheetah's 100 kilometres per hour!

Swimmers and divers

18 **Most swimming mammals have flippers and fins instead of legs.** Their bodies have become sleek and streamlined to help them move through the water easily. Seals and sea lions have large, paddle-like flippers which they can use to drag themselves along on land, as well as for swimming power in water. Whales never come to land. They swim by moving their tails up and down and using their front flippers to steer.

◄ The narwhal is one of the strangest looking whales. One of its teeth grows out through a hole in its upper lip to form a tusk that grows up to 2.7 metres long. The narwhal lives in the Arctic Ocean, and can grow up to 6.1 metres long.

19 **The killer whale can swim at 55 kilometres an hour.** A fierce hunter, it uses its speed to chase fast-swimming prey such as squid, fish and seals. It sometimes hunts in groups and will even attack other whales. Killer whales live in all the world's oceans. Despite their name, they are the largest of the dolphin family. They grow up to 10 metres long and weigh as much as 9000 kilograms.

This fin is called the dorsal fin. On an adult male whale this fin alone is taller than a man, growing up to 2 metres high.

◄ The bowhead whale, also called the Greenland Right whale, lives in the Arctic Ocean. It grows up to 20 metres long, feeding on tiny creatures that it gets from the water using filters in its mouth called baleen.

QUIZ

1. How deep can a Weddell seal dive?
2. What is the layer of fat on a seal's body called?
3. How fast can a killer whale swim?
4. How do whales move their tails when they swim?

1. 600 metres or more 2. Blubber
3. 55 kilometres an hour
4. Up and down

◄ The northern fur seal grows up to 1.8 metres long. It is unusual because its rear flippers are much larger for its size than other species of fur seal.

Weddell seal

▲ The harp seal lives in the Arctic Ocean. It grows to about the same size as a man, up to 1.9 metres. It feeds mainly on fish and shellfish, which it catches on long, deep dives.

20 The Weddell seal can dive deeper than any other seal. It goes down to depths of 600 metres or more in its search for cod and other fish. The Weddell seal can stay underwater for a long while, and dives of more than an hour have been timed. This seal lives in the icy waters of Antarctica. Its body is covered with a thick layer of fatty blubber which helps to keep it warm.

Fliers and gliders

21 **Bats are the only true flying mammals.** They zoom through the air on wings made of skin. These are attached to the sides of their body and supported by specially adapted, extra-long bones of the arms and hands. Bats generally hunt at night. During the day they hang upside down by their feet from a branch or cave ledge. Their wings are neatly folded at their sides or around their body.

▲ Fruit—eating bats, such as flying foxes, live in the tropics. They feed mostly on fruit and leaves.

22 **There are more than 950 different types of bat.** They live in most parts of the world, but not in colder areas. Bats feed on many different sorts of food. Most common are the insect-eating bats which snatch their prey from the air while in flight. Others feast on pollen and nectar from flowers. Flesh-eating bats catch fish, birds, lizards and frogs.

▲ True vampire bats feed only on the blood of other mammals!

23 **Flying lemurs don't really fly – they just glide from tree to tree.** They can glide distances of up to 130 metres with the help of flaps of skin at the sides of the body. When the flying lemur takes off from a branch it holds its limbs out, stretching the skin flaps so that they act like a parachute.

24 **Other gliding mammals are the flying squirrels and gliders.** All can glide from tree to tree, like the flying lemur, with the help of flaps of skin at the sides of the body. Flying squirrels live in North America and parts of Asia. Gliders are a type of possum and live in Australia and New Guinea.

I DON'T BELIEVE IT!

A vampire bat consumes about 26 litres of blood a year. That's about as much as the total blood supply of five human beings!

Life in snow and ice

25 The polar bear is the biggest land-based predator in the Arctic. It can run fast, swim well and even dives under the ice to hunt its main prey – ringed seals. It also catches seabirds and land animals such as the Arctic hare and reindeer. The polar bear's thick white fur helps to keep it warm – even the soles of its feet are furry.

26 The musk ox has a long shaggy outer coat to help it survive the arctic cold. A thick undercoat keeps out the damp. The musk ox eats grass, moss and lichen. In winter it digs through the snow with its hooves to reach its food.

27 Caribou, also known as reindeer, feed in Arctic lands. The land around the Arctic Ocean is called the tundra. In the short summer plenty of plants grow, the caribou eat their fill and give birth to their young. When summer is over the caribou trek up to 1000 kilometres south to spend the winter in forests.

28 The lemming builds its nest under the snow in winter. The nest is made on the ground from dry plants and twigs. The lemming makes tunnels under the snow from its nest to find grass, berries and lichen to eat. During the summer the lemming nests underground.

29 The walrus uses its long tusks for many tasks. They are used to drag itself out of water and onto the ice as well as for defending itself against enemies and rival walruses. The tusks can grow as much as 1 metre long.

30 The leopard seal is the fiercest hunter in the Antarctic. It lives in the waters around Antarctica and preys on penguins, fish and even other seals. There are no land mammals in the Antarctic.

Walrus

31 Some arctic animals such as the Arctic hare and the ermine, or stoat, change colour. In winter these animals have white fur which helps them hide among the snow. In summer, when white fur would make them very easy to spot, their coats turn brown.

Creatures of the night

32 **Not all mammals are active during the day.** Some sleep during the daylight hours and wake up at night. They are called nocturnal mammals, and there are many reasons for their habits. Bats, for example, hunt at night to avoid competition with daytime hunters, such as eagles and hawks. At night, bats and owls have the skies to themselves.

33 **The tarsier's big eyes help it to see in the dark.** This little primate lives in Southeast Asian forests where it hunts insects at night. Its big eyes help it make the most of whatever glimmer of light there is from the moon. Like the bats, it probably finds there is less competition for its insect prey at night.

◀ The western tarsier is only 16 centimetres long, but its huge tail can be up to 27 centimetres long.

34 **The red panda is a night feeder.** It curls up in a tree and sleeps during the day, but at night it searches for food such as bamboo shoots, roots, fruit and acorns. It also eats insects, birds' eggs and small animals. In summer, though, red pandas sometimes wake up in the day and climb trees to find fresh leaves to eat.

▼ Red pandas live in Asia, from the country of Nepal to Myanmar (Burma), and in Southwest China.

35 Hyenas come out at night to find food. During the day they shelter underground. Hyenas are scavengers – this means that they feed mainly on the remains of creatures killed by larger hunters. When a lion has eaten its fill, the hyenas rush in to grab the remains.

36 Bats hunt at night. Insect feeders, such as the horseshoe bat, manage to find their prey by means of a special kind of animal sonar. The bat makes high-pitched squeaks as it flies. If the waves from these sounds hit an animal, such as a moth, echoes bounce back to the bat. These echoes tell the bat where its prey is.

Large ears hear the echoes.

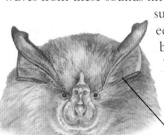

QUIZ

1. What do we call animals that come out only at night?
2. Where does the tarsier live?
3. What is a scavenger?
4. How does the horseshoe bat find its prey?
5. What does the red panda eat?

1. Nocturnal 2. Southeast Asia 3. An animal that eats the remains of creatures killed by larger hunters 4. By animal sonar 5. Bamboo shoots, fruit, acorns, insects, birds' eggs

21

Busy builders

37 **Beavers start their home building by damming a stream with branches, stones and mud.** They do this to make a deep, quiet lake where they can make a winter food store and a shelter called a lodge. Once the dam is made they begin to build the lodge, usually a dome-shaped structure made of sticks and mud. In summer, beavers feed on twigs, leaves and roots. They also collect extra branches and logs to store for the winter.

The beaver gnaws the tree to fell it and eat the soft bark.

The entrance to the lodge is usually underwater but the single chamber inside is above water level.

You can make your own mammal bookmark! Ask an adult to help you cut a piece of white card about 4 centimetres wide by 15 centimetres long. Draw a picture of a mammal onto your piece of card and colour it in. Now you have a mammal to help you read!

39 **The harvest mouse makes a nest on grass stems.** It winds some strong stems round one another to make a kind of platform. She then weaves some softer grass stems into the structure to form a ball-like shape about 10 centimetres across.

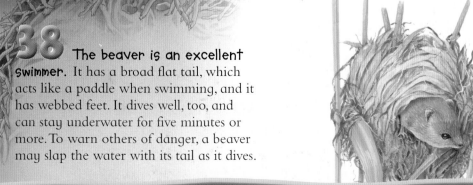

38 **The beaver is an excellent swimmer.** It has a broad flat tail, which acts like a paddle when swimming, and it has webbed feet. It dives well, too, and can stay underwater for five minutes or more. To warn others of danger, a beaver may slap the water with its tail as it dives.

Family life

40 Many mammals live alone, except when they have young, but others live in groups. Wolves live in family groups called packs. The pack is led by an adult female and her mate and may include up to 20 other animals.

41 Chimpanzees live in troops of anything from 15 to 80 animals. There are different types of troops, some are all male, some are just females with young, and some have males, females and young, led by an adult male. Each troop has its own territory which varies in size depending on how many animals are in the troop, and how far they need to travel for food. Troop bonds are loose and animals often move from one to another.

42 Lions live in groups called prides. The pride may include one or more adult males, females related to each other, and their young. The average number in a pride is 15. Female young generally stay with the pride of their birth but males must leave before they are full-grown. Lions are unusual in their family lifestyle – all other big cats live alone.

43 A type of mongoose called a meerkat lives in large groups of up to 30 animals. The group is called a colony and contains several family units of a pair of adults along with their young. The colony lives in a network of underground burrows. The members of the colony guard each other against enemies.

44 Naked mole rats live underground in a colony of animals led by one female. The colony includes about 100 animals and the ruling female, or queen, is the only one that produces young. Other colony members live like worker bees – they dig the burrows to find food for the group, and look after the queen.

45 Some whales live in families too. Pilot whales, for example, live in groups of 20 or more animals that swim and hunt together. A group may include several adult males and a number of females and their young.

46 The male elephant seal fights rival males to gather a group of females. This group is called a harem and the male seal defends his females from other males. The group does not stay together for long after mating.

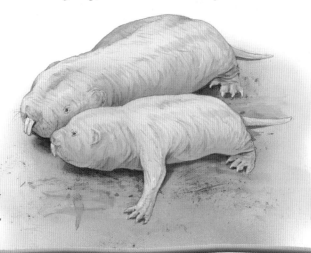

Desert dwellers

47 Many desert animals burrow underground to escape the scorching heat. The North African gerbil, for example, stays hidden all day and comes out at night to find seeds and insects to eat. This gerbil is so well adapted to desert life that it never needs to drink. It gets all the liquid it needs from its food.

▲ North African gerbil

48 The large ears of the fennec fox help it to lose heat from its body. This fox lives in the North African desert. For its size, it has the largest ears of any dog or fox.

Large ears also give the fennec fox very good hearing!

▼ Most camels are kept by people in the desert, but some still live wild.

49 A camel can last for weeks without drinking water. It can manage on the liquid it gets from feeding on desert plants. But when it does find some water it drinks as much as 80 litres at one time. It does not store water in its hump, but it can store fat.

50 The bactrian camel has thick fur to keep it warm in winter. It lives in the Gobi Desert in Asia where winter weather can be very cold indeed. In summer, the camel's long shaggy fur drops off, leaving the camel almost hairless.

51 **The kangaroo rat never needs to drink.** A mammal's kidneys control how much water there is in the animal's body. The kangaroo rat's kidneys are much more efficient than ours. It can even make some of its food into water inside its body!

▶ The kangaroo rat is named because it has long, strong back legs and can jump like a kangaroo.

QUIZ

1. How much water can a camel drink in one go?
2. Where does the bactrian camel live?
3. What dangerous animal does the desert hedgehog eat?
4. Which animals never need to drink?
5. Where does Pallas's cat live?

1. 80 litres 2. Gobi Desert
3. Scorpions 4. Kangaroo rat and the North African gerbil
5. The Gobi Desert

52 **The desert hedgehog eats scorpions as well as insects and birds' eggs.** It carefully nips off the scorpion's deadly sting before eating.

▲ The desert hedgehog digs a short, simple burrow into the sand. It stays there during the day to escape the heat.

53 **Pallas's cat lives in the Gobi Desert.** Its fur is thicker and longer than that of any other small cat to keep it warm in the cold Gobi winter. Pallas's cat lives alone, usually in a cave or a burrow and hunts small creatures such as mice and birds.

On the prowl

54 **Mammals which hunt and kill other creatures are called carnivores.** Examples of carnivores are animals such as lions, tigers, wolves and dogs. Meat is a more concentrated food than plants so many carnivores do not have to hunt every day. One kill will last them for several days.

▶ Most carnivores will hunt creatures smaller than themselves. The tiger can more easily catch and kill smaller prey like this water deer.

55 The tiger is the biggest of the big cats and an expert hunter. It hunts alone, often at night, and buffalo, deer and wild pigs are its usual prey. The tiger cannot run fast for long so it prefers to creep up on its prey without being noticed. Its stripy coat helps to keep it hidden among long grasses. When it is as close as possible to its prey, the tiger makes a swift pounce and kills its victim with a bite to the neck. The tiger clamps its powerful jaws around the victim's throat and suffocates it.

56 Bears eat many different sorts of food. They are carnivores but most bears, except for the polar bear, eat more plant material than meat. Brown bears eat fruit, nuts and insects and even catch fish. In summer, when salmon swim up rivers to lay their eggs, the bears wade into the shallows and hook fish from the water with their mighty paws.

MAKE A FOOD CHAIN

Make your own food chain. Draw a picture of a large carnivore such as a lion and tie it to a piece of string. Then draw a picture of an animal that the lion catches such as a zebra. Hang that from the picture of the lion. Lastly draw a picture of lots of grass and plants (the food of the zebra). Hang that from the picture of the zebra.

57 Hunting dogs hunt in packs. Together, they can bring down a much larger animal. The pack sets off after a herd of plant-eaters such as zebras or gazelles. They try to separate one animal that is perhaps weaker or slower from the rest of the herd.

Fighting back

58 **Some animals have special ways of defending themselves from deadly enemies.** The nine-banded armadillo protects itself with its body armour. Strong plates made of bone, topped with a layer of horn, cover the armadillo's back, sides and head. Its legs and belly are left unprotected, but if it is attacked the armadillo rolls itself up into tight ball.

▲ Nine-banded armadillo

59 **The skunk defends itself with a bad-smelling fluid.** This fluid comes from special glands near the animal's tail. If threatened, the skunk lifts its tail and sprays its enemy. The fluid's strong smell irritates the victim's eyes and makes it hard to breathe, and the skunk runs away.

60 **The porcupine's body is covered with as many as 30,000 sharp spines.** When an enemy approaches, the porcupine first rattles its spines as a warning. If this fails, the porcupine runs towards the attacker and drives the sharp spines into its flesh.

61 A rhinoceros may charge its enemies at top speed. Rhinoceroses are generally peaceful animals but a female will defend her calf fiercely. If the calf is threatened, she will gallop towards the enemy with her head down and lunge with her sharp horns. Few predators will stay around to challenge an angry rhino.

▲ The sight of a full-grown rhinoceros charging is enough to make most predators turn and run.

62 The pangolin's body is protected by tough overlapping scales. These make the animal look rather like a giant pinecone. The pangolin feeds mainly on ants and termites and its thick scales protect it from the stinging bites of its tiny prey.

Deep in the jungle

63 Jungle mammals live at all levels of the forest from the tallest trees to the forest floor. Bats fly over the tree tops and monkeys and apes swing from branch to branch. Lower down, smaller creatures, such as civets and pottos, hide among the dense greenery.

Moustached bat

Angwantibo

Pygmy chimpanzee

Gorilla

Talapoin

Jaguar

Giant armadillo

Civet

64 The jaguar is one of the fiercest hunters in the jungle. It lives in the South American rainforest and is the largest cat in South America. The pig-like peccary and the capybara – a large jungle rodent – are among its favourite prey.

65 The howler monkey has the loudest voice in the jungle. Each troop of howler monkeys has its own special area, called a territory. Males in rival troops shout at each other to defend their territory. Their shouts can be heard from nearly 5 kilometres away.

66 **The sloth hardly ever comes down to the ground.** This jungle creature lives hanging from a branch by its special hook-like claws. It is so well adapted to this life that its fur grows downwards – the opposite way to that of most mammals – so that rainwater drips off more easily.

Two-toed sloth

I DON'T BELIEVE IT!

The sloth is the slowest animal in the world. In the trees it moves along at only about 5 metres a minute. On the ground it moves even more slowly – about 2 metres a minute!

67 **Some monkeys, such as the South American woolly monkey, have a long tail that they use as an extra limb when climbing.** This is called a prehensile tail. It contains a powerful system of bones and muscles so it can be used for gripping.

68 **Tapirs are plump pig-like animals which live on the jungle floor.** There are three different kinds of tapir in the South American rainforests and one kind in the rainforests of Southeast Asia. Tapirs have long bendy snouts and they feed on leaves, buds and grass.

▼ This Brazilian tapir is often found near water and is a good swimmer.

69 **The okapi uses its long tongue to pick leaves from forest trees.** This tongue is so long that the okapi can lick its own eyes clean! The okapi lives in the African rainforest.

Strange foods

70 **Some mammals only eat one or two kinds of food.** The giant panda, for instance, feeds mainly on the shoots and roots of the bamboo plant. It spends up to 12 hours a day eating, and gobbles up about 12 kilograms of bamboo a day. The panda also eats small amounts of other plants such as irises and crocuses, and very occasionally hunts small creatures such as mice and fish. Giant pandas live in the bamboo forests of central China.

▼ People used to think that vampire bats sucked blood up through fangs. Now we know that they lap like a cat.

▲ There are very few giant pandas left in the world. Their homes are being cut down, which leaves them with nothing to eat.

71 **The vampire bat feeds only on blood – it is the only bat which has this special diet.** The vampire bat hunts at night. It finds a victim such as a horse or cow and crawls up its leg onto its body. The bat shaves away a small area of flesh and, using its long tongue, laps up the blood that flows from the wound. The vampire bat feeds for about 30 minutes, and probably drinks about 26 litres of blood a year.

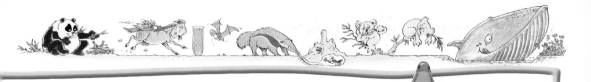

72 Tiny ants and termites are the main foods of the giant anteater. The anteater breaks open the insects' nests with its strong hooked claws. It laps up huge quantities of the creatures, their eggs and their young with its long tongue. This tongue is about 60 centimetres long and has a sticky surface that helps the anteater to catch the insects.

Giant anteater

QUIZ

1. From how far away can you hear a howler monkey?
2. How fast does a sloth move along the ground?
3. Some monkeys have tails they can grip with. What is the word for them?
4. How much bamboo does a giant panda eat in a day?
5. What does the koala eat?
6. How long is an anteater's tongue?

1. Nearly 5 kilometres 2. About 2 metres per minute 3. Prehensile 4. About 12 kilograms 5. Eucalyptus leaves 6. 60 centimetres

73 The mighty blue whale eats only tiny shrimp–like creatures called krill. The whale strains these from the water through a special filter system in its mouth called baleen. It may eat up to 4 tonnes of krill a day.

Baleen

74 The koala eats the leaves of eucalyptus plants. These leaves are very tough and can be poisonous to many other animals. They do not contain much goodness and the koala has to eat for several hours every day to get enough food. It spends the rest of its time sleeping to save energy. The koala's digestive system has adapted to help it cope with this unusual diet.

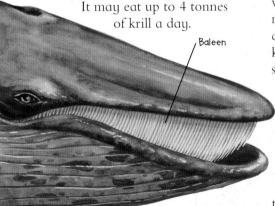

Tool users

75 **The chimpanzee is one of the few mammals to use tools to help it find food.** It uses a stone like a hammer to crack nuts, and uses sticks to pull down fruit from the trees and for fighting. It also uses sticks to help catch insects.

▶ The chimp pokes a sharp stick into a termite or ant nest. It waits a moment or two and then pulls the stick out, covered with juicy insects which it can eat.

▶ Chimps have also discovered that leaves make a useful sponge for soaking up water to drink or for wiping their bodies. Scientists think that baby chimps are not born knowing how to use tools. They have to learn their skills by watching adults at work.

76 The sea otter uses a stone to break open its shellfish food. It feeds mainly on sea creatures with hard shells, such as mussels, clams and crabs. The sea otter lies on its back in the water and places a rock on its chest. It then bangs the shellfish against the rock until the shell breaks, allowing the otter to get at the soft meat inside.

▲ The sea otter spends most of its life in the waters of the North Pacific and is an expert swimmer and diver.

77 The cusimanse is a very clever kind of mongoose. It eats frogs, reptiles, mammals and birds, but it also eats crabs and birds' eggs. When it comes across a meal that is protected by a tough shell, it throws it back between its hind legs against a stone or tree to break it open and get at the tasty insides!

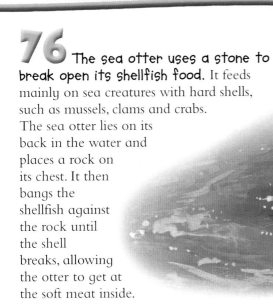

ANIMAL POSTERS

Take a sheet of paper and trace as many predators from this book as you can find. Colour them in and put a big heading – PREDATORS. Take another sheet and trace all the plant-eaters you can find. Put a big heading – PLANT-EATERS.

PREDATORS   PLANT-EATERS

City creatures

78 Foxes are among the few large mammals which manage to survive in towns and cities. Once foxes found all their food in the countryside, but now more and more have discovered that city rubbish bins are a good hunting ground. The red fox will eat almost anything. It kills birds, rabbits, eats insects, fruit and berries and takes human leavings.

79 Raccoons also live in city areas and raid rubbish bins for food. Like foxes, they eat lots of different kinds of food, including fish, nuts, seeds, berries and insects, as well as what they scavenge from humans. They are usually active at night and spend the day in a den made in a burrow, a hole in rocks or even in the corner of an empty city building.

80 Rats and mice are among the most successful of all mammals. They live all over the world and they eat almost any kind of food. The brown rat and the house mouse are among the most common. The brown rat eats seeds, fruit and grain, but it will also attack birds and mice. In cities it lives in cellars and sewers, anywhere there is rotting food and rubbish. The house mouse hides under floors and in cupboards. It will eat any human food it can find, as well as paper, glue and even soap!

I DON'T BELIEVE IT!

Rats will eat almost anything. They have been known to chew through electrical wires, lead piping and even concrete dams. In the United States rats are said to cause up to 1 billion dollars' worth of damage every year!

Fresh water mammals

81 **Most river mammals spend only part of their time in water.** Creatures such as the river otter and the water rat live on land and go into the water to find food. The hippopotamus, on the other hand, spends most of its day in water to keep cool. Its skin needs to stay moist, and it cracks if it gets too dry.

▶ The hippo is not a good swimmer but it can walk on the riverbed. It can stay underwater for up to half an hour.

82 **Webbed feet make the water rat a good swimmer.** They help the rat push its way through water. Other special features for a life spent partly in water include its streamlined body and small ears.

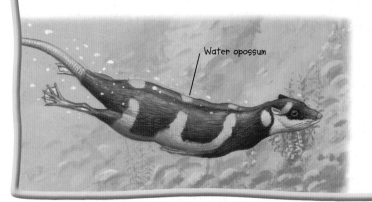

Water opossum

83 **The water opossum is the only marsupial that lives in water.** Found around lakes and streams in South America, it hides in a burrow during the day and dives into the river at night to find fish.

▼ When a platypus has found its food, it stores it in its cheeks until it has time to eat it.

84 **The platypus uses its duck–like beak to find food in the riverbed.** This strange beak is extremely sensitive to touch and to tiny electric currents given off by prey. The platypus dives down to the bottom of the river and digs in the mud for creatures such as worms and shrimps.

Eurasian otter

85 **The river otter's ears close off when it is swimming.** This stops water getting into them when the otter dives. Other special features are the otter's webbed feet, and its short, thick fur, which keeps its skin dry.

QUIZ

1. When are city foxes most active?
2. Do raccoons eat only seeds and berries?
3. What are the most common types of rats and mice?
4. Which is the only marsupial that lives in water?
5. What does the platypus eat?
6. Where do river dolphins live?
7. How does the water rat swim?

1. At night 2. No, they also eat fish, nuts and insects 3. Brown rats and house mice 4. Water opossum 5. Worms, shrimps and snails 6. Asia and South America 7. With the help of its webbed feet

86 **Most dolphins are sea creatures but some live in rivers.** There are five different kinds of river dolphins living in rivers in Asia and South America. All feed on fish and shellfish. They probably use echolocation, a kind of sonar like that used by bats, to find their prey.

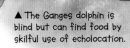

▲ The Ganges dolphin is blind but can find food by skilful use of echolocation.

Plant-eaters

87 Plant-eaters must spend much of their time eating in order to get enough nourishment. A zebra spends at least half its day munching grass. The advantage of being a plant-eater, though, is that the animal does not have to chase and compete for its food like hunters do.

▲ Carnivores, such as lions, feed on plant-eaters, so there must always be more plant-eaters than there are carnivores for this 'food chain' to work successfully.

Queensland blossom bat

88 Some kinds of bat feed on pollen and nectar. The Queensland blossom bat, for example, has a long brush-like tongue which it plunges deep into flowers to gather its food. As it feeds it pollinates the flowers – it takes the male pollen to the female parts of a flower so that it can bear seeds and fruits.

89

Rabbits have strong teeth for eating leaves and bark. The large front teeth are called incisors and they are used for biting leaves and chopping twigs. The incisors keep growing throughout the rabbit's life – if they did not they would soon wear out. Farther back in the rabbit's mouth are broad teeth for chewing.

90

The manatee is a water-living mammal which feeds on plants. There are three different kinds of these large, gentle creatures: two live in fresh water in West Africa and in the South American rainforest, and the third lives in the west Atlantic, from Florida to the Amazon.

Manatee

Dugong

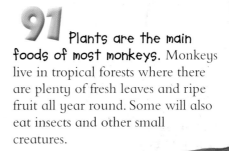

◄ Manatees, and their relations dugongs, feed on plants such as water weeds, water lilies and seaweeds.

91

Plants are the main foods of most monkeys. Monkeys live in tropical forests where there are plenty of fresh leaves and ripe fruit all year round. Some will also eat insects and other small creatures.

White-cheeked mangabey

Digging deep

92 **Champion burrowers of the mammal world are prairie dogs.** These little animals are not dogs at all but a kind of plump short-tailed squirrel. There are five different species, all of which live in North America. They live in large burrows, which contain several chambers linked by tunnels.

▲ A family of prairie dogs is called a coterie and contains about 8 animals – a male, several females and young. A large number of coteries live close to each other in huge colonies, called 'towns', which may cover hundreds of kilometres. Prairie dogs feed on grass and other plants.

93
Moles have specially adapted front feet for digging.
The feet are very broad and are turned outwards for pushing through the soil. They have large strong claws. The mole has very poor sight. Its sense of touch is very well developed and it has sensitive bristles on its face.

European mole

I DON'T BELIEVE IT!
Prairie dogs are not always safe in their own homes. Sometimes burrowing owls move into part of a burrow and then prey on the animals already living there.

94
Badgers dig a network of chambers and tunnels called a sett.
There are special areas in the sett for breeding, sleeping and food stores. Sleeping areas are lined with dry grass and leaves which the badgers sometimes take outside to air for a while.

▼ Badgers usually stay in the burrow during the day and come out at dusk. They are playful creatures and adults are often seen chasing and even leapfrogging with their cubs.

Mothers and babies

95 **Most whales are born tail first.** If the baby emerged head first it could drown during the birth process. As soon as the baby has fully emerged, the mother, with the help of other females, gently pushes it up to the surface to take its first breath. The female whale feeds her baby on milk, just like other mammals.

96 **The blue whale has a bigger baby than any other mammal.** At birth the baby is about 7 metres long and weighs 2000 kilograms – that's more than 30 average people. It drinks as much as 500 litres of milk a day!

Baby blue whale

97 **A baby panda weighs only about 100 grams at birth – that's about as big as a white mouse.** It is tiny compared to its mother, who may weigh 100 kilograms or more. The newborn cub is blind and helpless, with a thin covering of white fur. By four weeks it has black and white fur like an adult, and its eyes open when it is two to three months old. It starts to walk when it is about four months and begins to eat bamboo at six months.

98 Some babies have to be up and running less than an hour after birth. If the young of animals such as antelopes were as helpless as the baby panda they would immediately be snapped up by predators. They must get to their feet and be able to move with the herd as quickly as possible or they will not survive.

QUIZ

1. Where do prairie dogs live?
2. What is the name for the tunnels that badgers dig?
3. How much does a baby blue whale weigh?
4. How long is an elephant's pregnancy?
5. How many babies does the Virginia opossum have?
6. How much does a baby panda weigh?

1. North America 2. A sett 3. 2000 kilograms 4. 20–21 months 5. up to 21 babies 6. 100 grams

Virginia opossum

Babies in mother's pouch

99 The female elephant has the longest pregnancy of any mammal. She carries her baby for 20 to 21 months. The calf weighs about 100 kilograms when it is born. It can stand up soon after the birth and run around after its mother when it is a few days old.

100 The Virginia opossum has as many as 21 babies at one time – more than any other mammal. The young are only a centimetre long, and all of the babies together weigh only a couple of grams.

47

Index